A Guide to Creating Your Wellness Center

A Guide to Creating Your Wellness Center

PAULA K. JILANIS

iUniverse, Inc.
Bloomington

A Guide to Creating Your Wellness Center

iUniverse books may be ordered through booksellers or by contacting:

iUniverse
1663 Liberty Drive
Bloomington, IN 47403
www.iuniverse.com
1-800-Authors (1-800-288-4677)

ISBN: 978-1-4502-8862-0 (sc)
ISBN: 978-1-4502-8864-4 (dj)
ISBN: 978-1-4502-8863-7 (ebk)

Printed in the United States of America

iUniverse rev. date: 01/27/2011

This guidebook is dedicated to my parents,
who have given me life;

to my siblings,
in whose presence I know growth;

to my children,
in whose presence I know love;

to my grandchildren,
in whose presence I know joy; and

to my husband,
in whose presence I know partnership.

COMMITMENT
by Carey Elizabeth Smith

The willingness to stay engaged
in the face of obstacles,
dislikes, frustrations, disappointments, fears, judgments and a
relentless inner monologue that lists all the reasons to quit

A reaching into an even deeper longing to stay; a discipline to
see the project, assignment, relationship,
journey through to completion

A faithful return, again and again, to a threshold requiring
increased skill to move to the next level of understanding
or increased understanding to move to the next level of skill

A good day may be one step, the next breath
or just holding ground

I am

I do

I can

I shall

I choose

I commit

I am a commitment to

for the sake of ...

Contents

Acknowledgments

A deep bow of gratitude to the following people:

Bonnie and Gerry Kunkel, who offered their love, their home, and many cups of coffee so graciously during many weekends.

Cindi Pridgen, whose friendship I cherish and who listened for hours into the night about this process.

Rob Bastress, whose insight and understanding of the Five Element theory solidified this work for me.

Barb Buehl, whose executive background offered invaluable insight.

Marion Leonard, whose wisdom and challenges solidified this work.

Karen Smith, whose encouragement and knowledge of wellness clarified portions of this work.

Amy Schwab-Owens, whose understanding of wellness and emotional support was deeply felt.

Judy Pula and Jenna Gallion, for their editing work.

Karen Carrier, Dr. Wayne Jonas, Carter McNamara, Jon Robison, Carey Smith, and Cherie Sohnen-Moe, for their gracious willingness to share their materials.

The faculty at Tai Sophia Institute, who shared their wisdom and challenged my certitudes to help me see a wider vision of the world.

My family, whose encouragement buoyed me up and helped keep me afloat.

My husband, Gene, who loved and encouraged me through this process.

John Levering, whose drawings symbolizing the Five Elements were created for inclusion in *Traditional Acupuncture: The Law of the Five Elements* by Dianne M. Connelly (published by Tai Sophia Institute).

Introduction

For over ten years, I have had a dream of opening a wellness center. I would sit and dream about the location, the architecture of the building, the floor plan, and the colors for the various rooms. I would imagine myriad options for people to experience at this center. I eventually purchased over thirteen acres of woods in the Appalachian Mountains of western Maryland, with the idea of making my dream a reality. I set a plan in motion that included earning a master's degree in applied healing arts from Tai Sophia Institute in Columbia, Maryland.

During my education process, I was required to complete a final project as a capstone to my degree work. I chose a project that would tie into my dream of opening a wellness center. I began searching the Internet for information about starting a wellness center. I found many interesting and beautiful sites on actual wellness centers and what they offered, but I found nothing about the process of starting a wellness center. I found many traditional sites that taught how to start a business. However, I was looking for something more heartfelt and down to earth than traditional business start-up information. I wanted something that would take me through a personal process as well as educate me about starting a business. I found nothing. So this guidebook started out as my final project at Tai Sophia Institute. In that process, I discovered aspects of myself that I did not know existed. I hope that as you use this book, it becomes as path of self-discovery for you, as well.

We are living in exciting times. Our long-held certitudes about health care are changing. The mechanistic universe of the traditional biomedical model, in which the body is viewed as a machine, is being replaced by a more holistic and integrative model, in which the body is viewed as a dynamic energy system that works with and is affected by everything. We are no longer fighting disease (Robison and Carrier 2004). We are now creating health. New models of health promotion are being offered, and we are moving from positions of opposition, where physicians dictate our course of action, to positions of partnerships, whereby we work together in preventive ways to address our health.

With the world economy in its present state, we are all looking for ways to cut costs. The high costs of doctors' visits, prescriptions, and procedures are strongly encouraging us, if not forcing us, to explore new methods of health care delivery. Assuming a greater role in our own health and wellness is perhaps the most effective way to empower us. The preventive aspect inherent in such a posture may also help lessen the rising role that finances are playing in health care choices. Additionally, a preventive view of health and wellness, rather than a reactive (illness/disease) view, empowers us both individually and as community.

"Health" and "wellness" are two terms that have been used interchangeably for many years. They are increasingly viewed as partners in our lives rather than adversaries. For me, health is defined as living the best I can day to day, given my physical, emotional, mental, and spiritual life. Here are a few classic definitions of health and wellness:

1. "Health is not freedom from the inevitability of death, disease, unhappiness, and stress, but rather the ability to cope with them in a competent way" (Illich 1976).
2. "Health can be redefined as the manner in which we live well despite our inescapable illnesses, disabilities, and trauma" (Morris 2007).

3. "Wellness is an attitude and an app   king toward
   integration of physical, mental, emo   nd spiritual
   well-being, leading to a richer quality   in 2003).

4. "Wellness is the integration, balance,   of mind,
   body, spirit, and emotions that leads   l-being,
   where the whole is greater than the sum   :award
   2001).

We are coming to a greater understanding of   : of
our relationship to the world and to all aspects of ou   iur
connectedness. To me, wellness is my attitude rega   re
my life and how I bring all of its many aspects int   s
integration.

Our bodies work naturally to maintain balance. It
of balance and move away from our true nature, our b
messages to call us back to that balance. "If we don't get t
in subtle ways, our bodies will start to speak more loudly ur
it" (Hay 1987). "We must take time to listen because how w
our health has a direct impact on our health" (Idel and Kasl 1991).

One of the ways for us to listen to our bodies is to remember that
we are connected to and are a part of nature. A recent study found that
a brief walk in a natural environment can actually improve memory
performance and attention span (Weil 2009). When we take advantage
of our connection with nature and the elements, we can listen to our
bodies and know better what is required.

Just as the rivers, streams, oceans, and seas are the life force for
nature, chi is the life force for humanity. It is the energy that is in all
living things. It is the core tenet of traditional Chinese medicine. It is
what keeps us alive, what helps us to grow, and also what helps us to
die. Moreover, just as the seasons come and go in cycles, so too do we
cycle through life. Our life cycles are as connected to the changes in
the seasons as the earth itself is. So therefore, we must acknowledge the
human connection to the earth.

This manual explores starting a wellness center through the lens of traditional Chinese medicine's Five Element theory. Traditional Chinese medicine was originally an oral tradition of health and wellness, with information passed down by the ancients in parables and teaching stories. Customarily, the body is described as the kingdom, and the heart is its emperor/empress. All the major organs are described poetically as officials with defined tasks to support the kingdom. The major organs of the body are connected with each of the seasons, which coincide with one of the five elements: water, wood, fire, earth, and metal. How can we have five elements with only four seasons? In the Five Element theory, there are five seasons. The fifth season is late summer and correlates with the element of earth. It starts in late August when the season starts to change. For this book, the theory has been used to explore the facets of establishing a business. Utilizing this metaphor of the elements and the seasons is a fitting model for creating a well-rounded, holistic wellness center.

The chapters of this manual are broken up into major categories that match the Five Elements of traditional Chinese medicine. Each will include a short explanation of the characteristics of the element, its season, and its virtues.

My choice in utilizing the Five Element theory has come from my master's degree work at Tai Sophia Institute. Through the use of this theory, I have found new and easier ways of exploring aspects of business that I find challenging. When I teach, I work best when I can bring in the relationship components, and the Five Element theory helps me do that. I have been able to examine various components of business through the lens of the qualities and characteristics of each of the elements. Using the concepts of the Five Element theory has helped me bring business to life, a topic that I find difficult. For those of you who are more relational and less linear, you may find this beneficial.

This manual addresses all of the major requirements for beginning a center. However, using the characteristics of the Five Element theory provides a connection and groundedness to the earth that too often are missing in our linear Western planning methods. This guidebook is meant to be a key reference resource in your planning process. It is dynamic and adaptable, but it is not intended to be an all-inclusive manual. It will allow you to incorporate your personal touches and individual ideas. It is offered as a gift from my heart to suit your needs.

Water

Water Element

for whatever we lose (like a you or a me),
it's always ourself we find in the sea.
—e. e. cummings

The water element is an expression of the season of winter. Within it lies the control of potency and power. It calls for deep listening to and learning in the unknowing. It asks us to look into ourselves, literally and figuratively, build our inner resources, face our fears, and embrace our inner courage. It requires that we examine the greatness of who we truly are. Like the medium itself, all aspects of our lives must coexist in a fluid and flowing state.

The water element gives us the capacity to conserve and store our vital energy. The virtues of patience, conservation, and restraint are embodied therein. What measure do we use to set limits and to conserve energy? "We are reminded of the necessity of restraint and containing ourselves to serve life. In this season, we see the generation of power, strength, and the will to [live]" (Balles 2004).

Water is symbolic of the courage to move forward in the face of adversity. The characteristics of strength, power, and perseverance are also present with us in this season of winter. From here, we explore what steps we need to take despite our fears.

When examining the concept of a wellness center, the water element directs us to take stock of ourselves. We have to take into account all internal and external reserves. We must look honestly at our personal desire to achieve the goal of establishing a center and then balance that desire against a sense of courage and restraint. What are the unknowns that must be explored? Within the confines of the water element, and under any of the following elements for that matter, determine your true readiness to create a wellness center. Look at what similar facilities and programs already exist and the viability of your proposed venture. In this element, you will start to move from the unknowing to the knowing.

Chapter 1

Am I Ready for This?

Before writing this guidebook, my answer to this question would have been an instantaneous "yes" without any thought. At times, I can believe things are possible without completely thinking through the process. The intent of this chapter is to help us explore some of the questions that may be missed.

In creating a wellness center, before we can start exploring the outside resources, we can benefit from first exploring our own inner resources. It is helpful to know whether we are truly ready to start this adventure. It is also helpful to examine our strengths and understand our challenges.

There are many methods for self-exploration. In this guidebook, I will offer two methods. The first method allows us to explore ourselves through the Five Elements. The second method is a more traditional method of exploration. Whether the reasons seem purely pragmatic or deeply esoteric, we are starting on a new journey of self-discovery.

As we begin this exploration, I suggest that we take time in quiet, in that place of deep listening and stillness, to allow our true inner voice to be heard.

Some of the following questions have been adapted from the book *Dancing with Ten Thousand Things* by Tom Balles (2004). For each of the Five Elements I have answered some of the questions to "prime the pump" for you in addressing the questions.

Winter Water Element

What do you know about yourself?
> I know that I am great at getting things started, and that once things are up and running, I am ready to move on and start another endeavor.

What don't you know about yourself?
What is your level of patience?
Of what are you afraid?
> I am afraid that the business will not get off the ground and I will lose all of my investment, and then people will laugh at me.

How resourceful are you?
What is your internal voice saying?
> This one is easy. There is one voice that says, "This is great, let's finally get this thing going." There is another voice (that internal gremlin) that says I am going to fail. This voice I have to keep in check.

What are others saying to you?
Where do you get your courage and sense of power?

Spring Wood Element

What is your long-range vision?
> My long-range vision is to create a center that will have several components. It will be a resource center to give people in the community wellness information. It will offer classes, seminars, and workshops in all dimensions of wellness. It will have practitioners from several different disciplines who will work together as a team to address clients' issues and develop wellness plans for individual clients.

What decisions need to be made now?

Can you hold your ground in a conflict?

>My answer for this is it depends. If I believe that a boundary is being violated, I can hold my ground; for instance, if a client arrives twenty minutes late for an appointment and still expects a full session, I can hold my ground. However, if I am not clear about my position, I may not hold my ground as well.

How are you at cutting through the chaff to be direct?

What steps are you taking to achieve your goal?

Do you see yourself growing in this process?

Is the timing right for this?

How do you experience creativity flowing?

>I find that I go in spurts. Once the creativity starts to flow, I want to stick with it. I can be a procrastinator. I have started to recognize that I think about things for quite a while before I sit down to the computer. So I am not really procrastinating, rather I am processing internally before I put my fingers to keys.

Summer Fire Element

With whom can you partner?

For the sake of whom or what will you start this endeavor?

>When I looked at this question, I really discovered something about myself. In some cases, doing something for my own sake did not light a passion within me to complete the task. When I began to explore doing something for the sake of a family member or a particular group of people, the passion and commitment rose from my core. Starting this center will be done for the sake of my grandchildren.

Do you need to clear something out before you can start?

Are you certain about what belongs and what does not belong?

How are your levels of communication?

>My levels of communication are clear, unless my emotions get involved. Sometimes I must step back to separate what I feel

about the situation and what I know about the situation. For me, I have learned that I must keep my emotions in check when I am communicating in the business world.

Do you need training on how to build communication bridges?

Does this touch your heart?

Late Summer Earth Element

Is there someone with whom you can share responsibilities?

> This is one question that I have to sit and think about to answer. As the oldest of five children, I was given responsibilities at a very young age, so I know how to be responsible. I feel much more challenged to delegate responsibilities with another person. Yet, I know this venture will fail if I attempt to do it all alone.

Have you built in time for reflection?

Are you operating from the mentality of lack or of abundance?

> I am constantly working at maintaining the attitude of abundance. I know there are times where I do slip back into a mentality of lack. I think the key is to be gentle with myself when I do slip.

What are your thoughts and ideas around gratitude for this opportunity?

Autumn Metal Element

What gives you inspiration for this wellness center?

What thoughts, ideas, or concepts do you need to release or let go?

> I need to let go of judging myself, and I need to release my doubts about creating this wellness center. I want to hold onto the thoughts, ideas, and concepts of the center as a success rather than as a failure.

What do you need to acknowledge just as it is?

Is there any area of this creation or inspiration where you feel stifled or suffocated?

The following is a more traditional method of exploration. For some of us, this is a necessary part of the process. Using one or both processes can be very helpful.

A. Take inventory of where you are professionally and personally.
1) List your educational achievements.
2) List your accomplishments.
3) List your growing edges/weaknesses.
4) List five areas where you are a beginner.
5) List things you like to do.
6) List things you have mastered or overcome personally and professionally.
7) List your system of support.
8) List your family and friends' emotional backing and support.
9) What things are working?
10) Where do things need to change?
11) What things may be in the way of starting a business?
12) *If I could be anywhere, doing anything, where would it be and what would I be doing?*

B. Evaluate your readiness for self-employment.
1) In what ways are you motivated—a self-starter?
2) Are you better at getting things started or at maintaining what has been started?
3) What is your attitude toward money?
4) Do you have the required skills to run a business?
5) In what ways are you a leader?
6) Do you like to work solo or are you more of a collaborative worker?
7) Do you follow through with what you say you will do?
8) How well do you organize what you need to accomplish?
9) Do you procrastinate or do you make decisions quickly?

10) Is your health/energy high enough to put in the long hours required?
11) Are you are a leader or a follower?
12) Do you like to take risks?
13) Create a plan.

Now you are standing on firm ground, knowing what resources are available for you and identifying those that are missing.

Next Step

You are ready to take the next step. You will want to set your goals and create a strategic plan for yourself. This will take some time, but it will be well worth the process. There is a basic business guideline for setting your goals and creating your strategic plan. In business terms, your goals need to be SMART: Specific, Measurable, Attainable, Realistic, and Timely. Let's look at each term. Be sure to make your goal specific. What do you want to accomplish? What are your reasons for doing it? Making a goal measurable helps to make the goal concrete. What will you use to measure your goals? Measuring your progress in concrete terms allows you to see your progress and assess your accomplishments. In measuring whether your goal is attainable, you will start to see the reality of your dream and where you may need to do some revamping. Is what you want to create realistic given the parameters your resources and support? This is where you look at how realistic your goals and your plan are at this time in your life. Everything may seem to be in place for you to begin this endeavor. However, is the timing right for it? Given all the various dimensions of your life, is what you want to create possible at this time?

You should also consider your life purpose and your priorities. You can examine these factors by breaking your plan down into a life plan, five-year plan, three-year plan, and so on. When you have a sense of these parts of your life, you can more effectively prepare a strategic plan.

A strategic plan takes this process, which may feel overwhelming and insurmountable, and chunks it down into pieces that are more manageable. When you create your strategic plan, you will want to include the following information: What do you want to accomplish? What is your goal? What is its purpose? Then list the priorities that originate from that goal. Next describe the situation, define the major goal, list the benefits of achieving the goal, brainstorm possible courses of action, and choose the best alternative outline—include the advantages, list the potential conflicts and solutions, identify resources needed, and outline the specific steps necessary to achieve the goal.

Using this process, you can take it one step at a time and feel like things are manageable. Next you need to learn what is required by your state and local authorities. Each state's requirements vary. You can check this website for information: www.business.gov. It has much of the information you will need to get started. It can tell you where to go to get information for your particular state.

Chapter 2

What Already Exists?

When starting any endeavor, it is important to find out whether there is already a facility like the one you want to start so you do not "reinvent the wheel." In the water element, it is important to be still and listen. Be sure to take the time to listen to learn what resources are already out there. A good place to start is with your local chamber of commerce or small business development group. They will have a great deal of information regarding what resources are currently available in your area. They can also tell you what services are missing in your community.

You may also want to go to the local United Way and local health department. They can provide information about what other types of programs are available; you might be able to create great partnerships for your center.

The YMCA, community groups such as adventure clubs, and your local gyms might be able to give you insight about the needs of the community. Traveling to various facilities to explore what is available and what is possible can be great fun. You may be interested in creating a high-end wellness center and be excited to find out that your community appears to need that kind of facility. Be sure to check into the reasons that type of facility does not already exist. It may be that no one in the community has thought of it. However, it could also be the fact that the socio-economic makeup of your area may not support it. Be sure to do your homework. You certainly would not want to open a facility and have it sit empty because the community is unable to support it.

To look at this metaphorically, you are in the home of health and wellness, looking around the rooms and taking inventory. You are finding out what is currently available to the community and what is missing. Does the community already have health and wellness centers? If so, what is missing from them? Are they focused on health and fitness? Are they missing the holistic wellness component, which addresses mind, body, and spirit? What type of activities and services do they offer? Are there services that are missing that would fit well into what you would like to develop in your center?

If the center that you want to create is similar to another business in the area, how is yours going to be different? What will draw clientele to your business rather than to your competitors? By exploring what already exists in your area, you may discover a niche that you can create. You may want to have a center that focuses on a specific group, such as women or families, or a specific health condition such as post surgery rehabilitation. You may want to create one that draws a certain demographic. You may want to offer outdoors wellness activities such as bike rides or hikes.

You can hone your dream by researching what is currently available in your community, assessing the demographics of the area, and determining the realistic possibilities of your center.

Chapter 3

Financial Considerations

Investment Partners

If you are fortunate enough to have people who are interested in being partners in your center, you should contract with a financial specialist as well as with a lawyer. These people can make sure that you protect all angles of the investment. Even if you are entering this endeavor solo, it is smart business sense to partner with a good financial specialist and a good lawyer to protect yourself and your business.

What Are the Risks?

It is imperative that you consider all possible risks. These include, but are not limited to, changes in the demand for your services, a recession, new competition, or changes in legislation. Be sure to have a contingency plan in place so you can weather the storm.

When examining your financial stability, many areas must be taken into account. Estimate the income you will generate for services offered to your clients, and look at these risks from several areas: employees' salaries and your portion of taxes as employer, supplies, and equipment needed for the next year.

Financial Management

This issue is vital for the success of any business. Attention to detail is a definite asset in this arena. Maintaining accurate daily, monthly, quarterly, and annual records and reports will make the process much easier when preparing for tax time. If your business is small, the recordkeeping obviously will be simpler than if you own a corporation.

A good rule of thumb for any business is to keep *all* receipts, maintain accurate daily logs, and be sure to pay your bills on time. There are several computer programs that are excellent for this documentation. (Many small businesses use QuickBooks.) These programs enable you to write checks and prepare reports online. All you need to do is enter the information. Your small business development group can recommend an efficient software program.

Here are some basics to remember: Be sure to have a separate checking and savings account for your business. Keep all business records for at least seven years (these include but are not limited to *all* business-related receipts, bank statements and monthly reconciliation records, ledgers, tax returns, any disbursements, credit card records, accounts receivable information, as well as profit-and-loss information). Of course, it is crucial to maintain client files securely. Other types of records to maintain are inventory lists for equipment and supplies, logs for automobile mileage, and daily records such as appointment books.

Income

We often think of income coming in the form of cash, but there are other ways to be paid. In today's world, it is convenient to allow your clients to pay using a credit or debit card. However, most credit card companies charge a monthly fee for this service. So be sure to shop around for the best deal for your business and decide whether you want to incur that monthly expense. If you offer gift certificates, be sure to check your state's regulations regarding the time frame allowed for honoring them. Some states require that you honor gift certificates longer than one year. Another consideration for your business: are you interested in bartering for services (cleaning, accounting, etc.)? This type of arrangement is also considered as income and therefore must be reported at tax time. If you choose to barter, be clear at the beginning and have the arrangement in writing. This will avoid any problems if the other person does not keep up with the arrangement.

Taxes

Check with your state tax office and the local small business development group. They can give you a great deal of information to ensure you comply with all tax laws. Also check with a tax lawyer; the IRS website (www.irs.gov/businesses/index.html) offers a checklist for businesses.

Documentation

If you are not a detail-oriented person or conscientious about maintaining records, you may want to hire someone who is gifted in this area. It can't be stressed enough how important good recordkeeping is to a successful business. The websites listed below offer free, reproducible forms. Some forms are included in this book's appendix as samples. They are good resources for making sure that you have the necessary areas covered for your business. Below are listed a few possibilities for exploring, using, and creating forms:

www.irs.gov/businesses/small/article/0,,id=99200,00.html
www.businessnation.com/library/forms
www.businessmastery.us/forms.php

Wood

Wood Element

I am not bound by any public place,
but for the ground of my own where I
have planted vines and orchard trees,
and in the heat of the day climb into
the healing shadows of the woods.
—Wendell Berry

The gifts of the wood element, associated with the season of spring, offer us strategy and planning. Its function is to open us to options and to take steps forward. After winter's time of building reserves, we are now ready to let fresh, clear energy flow. We are now rooted in ourselves. We can see the vision of what can be. From here we can see how we want to be in the world. Here we do our strategic planning, offer wise judgment, and make our decisions.

The season of spring reflects how well we can hold our ground. Flexibility, organization, and order are reflected in the spring, along with our capacity to be assertive and creative. The wood element of spring embodies boldness, benevolence, and vision (Balles 2004).

Our ability to make decisions and be firm and clear resides in the spring. If there is a way to get things done, we will see it through this season. Spring can see things across time. It is exact and direct.

From this season is expressed fairness, clarity, and decisiveness (Balles 2004).

In this section, we will delve into the vision for the center. Consider what you want the center to look like; also determine how you want the center to feel as someone enters the space. How do you want this center to "be" in the world?

Chapter 4

Vision and Mission Statements

What Are Vision and Mission Statements?

Vision and mission statements act as the philosophical foundation for your wellness center. Your center's vision statement is an umbrella statement; it needs to be strong enough and broad enough to last. Some people say the vision is an ideal. Others say it needs to be a realistic concept for your business. The mission statement gives more details about the purpose of your business.

A vision statement presents, in one line, how you want your center to be seen. It is a snapshot of your company. Below are listed some examples:

Samueli Institute (Alexandria, Virginia): *Our vision is a world in which healing is the formative concept for achieving and maintaining wellness and ameliorating chronic disease.*

Community Wellness Coalition (Cumberland, Maryland): *Community Wellness Coalition supports and empowers our community in creating a dynamic culture of wellness.*

The mission statement flows from the vision statement. A mission statement adds explanatory details about your company. It says who you are, what you do, and why you do what you do. In about a hundred words, it tells people the essence or spirit of your organization. It describes the action that flows from your vision. If a mission statement is longer than about one hundred words, it can become too confusing. People will stop reading it. One of the primary functions of your mission statement is to define who and what you are as a wellness center.

A properly created mission statement takes time for thought and discussion. You need time for introspection and clarity to create thoughtful expressions and make careful analyses. Quite often, creating a mission statement takes many rewrites to express the core of the company's vision.

Once you have your mission statement, you can use it to undergird all your actions. It is a good method for checks and balances. Before starting a new endeavor or partnership, you can ask yourself, "Does this align with our mission statement?" The mission statement also allows the public to measure how closely you conform to the mission.

What Should Your Statement Say?

Your mission statement is a broad, clear statement about your organization. It should explain who you are (name) and what do you do (focus). How will your center be different—eliminate traditional health care, provide greater awareness of wellness issues, or some other distinction? It should also explain why you are doing what you do (purpose). Listed below are two examples:

Samueli Institute: *The mission of the Samueli Institute is to transform health care through the scientific exploration of healing.*

Community Wellness Coalition: *The Community Wellness Coalition is dedicated to inform and inspire our community about an integrative approach to wellness. We promote and collaborate with individuals, groups, and organizations to enhance wellbeing and quality of life.*

The essence of the individual organization should be clear to the reader from each of these statements. In addition, members of the board can easily share these mission statements with the people in the community.

Just as organizations change and grow over time, it is possible that your mission statement may change. However, changes should not be made lightly. You will want to ask this question: Are you changing the mission statement because the organization's emphasis has truly changed, or are you being pushed to change by an influential member of the community or by a particular board member with a personal agenda? It is crucial that your mission and the actions of the organization are in sync.

Chapter 5

Profit/Nonprofit

The choice of creating a for-profit or a nonprofit business is a big decision. There are many issues to be examined. Both profit and nonprofit organizations must make a profit to be successful. The difference in the two types of business is in what happens to the profits. In a nonprofit organization, all the profits are reinvested back into the organization. In a for-profit organization, some of the profits are returned to owners or shareholders and some may be reinvested back into the business. The way your board of directors is established and how it functions differs: in this chapter, there is a chart that compares the boards of directors of for-profit and nonprofit businesses. The chart can also be found at www.managementhelp.org/boards/boards. htm#anchor98036, which is a good resource. Find a good lawyer who specializes in working with for-profit or nonprofit organizations as well as a lawyer who specializes in business law. These two professionals are a must for any business.

Of course, the US Small Business Administration (www.sba.gov/index.html) is also an excellent resource for information and help.

Profit

A for-profit organization is just that—a company that is in business to make a profit. If you choose to take this approach, you need to decide what type of legal structure you want for the business. There are four major legal entities: sole proprietorships, partnerships, limited liability companies (LLCs), and corporations. Corporations then have different categories (C corporations and S corporations). Let's look at each one individually.

Sole Proprietorships

This arrangement would be an option if you are working by yourself or with your spouse. If you have a co-owner of your business, the IRS requires you to set up at least a partnership.

The advantage to a proprietorship is that this type of business is usually easy to start up. Of course, you must check with your state regarding the licensing and legal requirements for starting a business, which can vary from state to state. Business decisions are made fairly easily when you do not need the approval of another person or a board of directors. As a sole proprietor, you file a Schedule C with your 1040 federal tax form, and profits are yours after expenses have been paid.

There are several disadvantages to a sole proprietorship. All debts and liabilities fall directly to you. They are your personal liability. You may have difficulty in getting financing. If there is a lawsuit, you could lose everything if the court rules against you (you could have to pay the claim from your personal assets).

Partnerships

Being in business with another individual can certainly ease the burden of ownership. If you decide to work in a partnership, it is imperative that you prepare a written agreement. A jointly owned business requires you to have discussions with your partner, which you would not need to do as a sole proprietor. For example, if you work alone, there is no need to decide who is responsible for cleaning or restocking shelves. This may seem to be a mundane task until there is a complaint when something was not done. So you may want to choose a partner who has similar goals and philosophies to facilitate decisions, which will help you succeed and expand your business.

Partnerships are very similar to sole proprietorships from the standpoint of government regulations. You must contact the IRS to complete an SS-4 form, which furnishes you with an employer identification number (EIN). Instead of completing a Schedule C form, partners complete a K-1 form, declaring the losses or profits on their 1040 form. As with a sole proprietorship, you are still not protected from personal liability.

Limited Liability Companies

This type of business is somewhat of a hybrid. It blends the profit sharing of a partnership and offers the personal liability protection of a corporation. Members can only be held accountable for liability if they sign a personal guarantee.

Like partnerships and sole proprietorships, the tax filing requirements are not complicated. LLC members file an IRS 1065 form along with their K-1 form, and members report their portion of profit or loss from the company.

Corporations

Corporations are the most regulated of the business entities. They are also the most costly to establish; documentation must be filed with the state, and fees have to be paid. There are state and federal requirements for maintaining documents, and certain reports must be developed, filed, and maintained. Corporations generally have shareholders, a board of directors, and officers. The board does not oversee the day-to-day management of the corporation but is responsible for making the major decisions. If you are interested in starting a corporation, it is advisable to contact legal counsel that specializes in this area of the law in your region.

C Corporations and S Corporations

C corporations and S corporations are similar in their limited liability protection, their establishment protocol, the responsibilities of their boards, their bylaws, and their requirements of holding annual shareholder meetings and filing annual reports.

C corporations are taxed as a corporation. In contrast, S corporations have to file a tax return. However, they are not required to pay taxes on their profits because the profits are issued as dividends to the shareholders, who then pay income tax. The advantage of this is that the profit is only taxed once.

Nonprofit

If you decide to form a nonprofit company, retain legal advice with a firm that works with nonprofit organizations.

First, have a discussion with your potential partners. With their experience, they may add information to the discussion that could be important in making your decision. If you decide that a nonprofit is a good fit, the US Department of Agriculture's website (www.rurdev.usda.gov) is a good resource for learning how to start a not-for-profit (enter "501(c)(3)" in the site's toolbox).

Completing the 501(3)(c) application allows a nonprofit company to receive tax-exempt status. When a nonprofit company submits a proposal for grant money, a copy of its 501(c)(3) designation is usually required.

On the website of the Charitable Organization Division of the Maryland Secretary of State (www.sos.state.md.us/Charity/

ChecklistNonProfit.pdf), you can download a checklist of the items you need to complete.

There is also great assistance available from Maryland Nonprofits (www.marylandnonprofits.org), which provides training for many aspects of nonprofit organizations. For other states, you can usually go to the state government's website and find sites to assist you.

Here is a comparison of For-Profit and Nonprofit corporations that may help clarify some questions (this is from www.managementhelp. org/misc/Nonprofits-ForProfits.pdf):

Comparison between For-Profit and Nonprofit Corporations

For-Profit Corporations	Nonprofit Corporations
Owned by stockholders	Owned by the public
Generate money for the owners	Serve the public
Success is making sizeable profit	Success is meeting needs of the public
Board members are usually paid	Board members are usually unpaid volunteers
Members can make very sizeable income	Members should make reasonable, not excessive, income
Money earned over and above that needed to pay expenses is kept as profit and distributed to owners	Money earned over and above that needed to pay expenses is retained as surplus and should be spent soon on meeting the public need (the nonprofit can earn profit from activities not directly related to the nonprofit's mission; however, the nonprofit often has to pay taxes over a certain amount)
Chief Executive Officer is often on the Board of Directors and sometimes is the President of the Board	Conventional wisdom suggests that the Chief Executive Officer (often called the "Executive Director") not be on the Board

For-Profit Corporations	Nonprofit Corporations
Usually not exempt from paying federal, state/provincial, and local taxes	Can often be exempt from federal taxes, and some state/provincial and local taxes, if the nonprofit was granted tax-exempt status from the appropriate governmental agency
Money invested in the for-profit usually cannot be deducted from the investor's personal tax liability	Money donated to the nonprofit can be deducted from the donor's personal tax liability if the nonprofit was granted charitable status from the appropriate government agency

Used with permission from Carter McNamara Authenticity Consulting.

Board of Directors/Board of Trustees

If you chose a for-profit corporation or a nonprofit business, you are required to put a board of directors (or trustees) in place to meet legal obligations. In both cases, the board is responsible for overseeing the workings of the business. They have fiscal and legal responsibility for the organization.

It is important that the composition of your board be diverse. One of the members should be an accountant, and one should be a legal counsel. Also, select people who are known in the community and who can support the institution financially. It is important to have a gender-balanced board. Include a consumer as a member of the board to bring in the perspective of the general public.

When selecting board members for a nonprofit organization, you will want to consider the following: How much time will they have to work on the board and help raise necessary funds? Especially in the early stages, you will need people who can help your business flourish. Board members have various functions in various committees. And a major responsibility, in addition to fiscal and legal responsibilities, is to raise funds for the organization.

Appoint board members who are in a financial position to support the business. Most people have favorite causes that they support. Wealthy people often ask their friends, other wealthy people, to assist with causes. If at some point you choose to submit a grant proposal, most foundations will look at the generosity of your board members. If a foundation sees that the board does not support your organization, it will raise a red flag when they evaluate your proposal.

You also want to choose board members with business savvy and good judgment. When it comes down to making decisions for the organization, you want people who have wisdom. Are they thoughtful, or do they fly by the seat of their pants?

Fire

Fire Element

The sun challenges the morning's cool moon.
The dance has begun!
—David M. Bell

For the gifts of the fire element, we are in the season of summer, where we explore partnerships. In this season, we get fired up and enthusiastic, and we flourish and grow. In the Five Element theory, this is the minister of the awakened heart. This is where we examine with whom we want to connect. We explore how we can have a win/win situation. From here we also offer the gift of the heart.

From the summer emanates compassion. All points of view are examined. In this season are demonstrated insight, responsibility, compassion, and understanding (Balles 2004).

Through the summer, sorting is done. Here we separate what works from what doesn't work, the pure from the impure. We refine from here. Summer embodies the virtues of discrimination and appropriateness (Balles 2004).

Through this fire element of summer are exuded job, love, and passion. This season also demonstrates intimacy, protection, and the lightness of being.

From here balance and harmony are maintained. The fire element of summer makes sure there is communication within and among all. All feel at home—"the hostess with the mostest." The season of summer is accepting, is gracious, and builds bridges between people (Balles 2004).

For your wellness center, the exploration now deals with the people aspects of the business. What people do you want to support you and participate with you in this process? Next we will explore what type of people you want to come to the center. What group do you want to serve? We will also examine the types of people you want to work at your center.

Chapter 6

Who Will Partner with You?

Choosing the right people to partner with can be a challenge. Some people are very practiced at being loners when it comes to taking on a new endeavor. If you are one of these people, this is an opportunity to learn how to be a partner. As I mentioned earlier, I can have the attitude of "I can do it myself." This type of attitude can be deadly in the business arena. Working alone sets up the possibility for leaving out or missing vital elements to the process. It is crucial to have varied perspectives as well as having more than one set of eyes and ears to examine the various aspects of the business. The more diversified the circle of partnerships and support is, the greater the likelihood of success.

Many businesses and organizations can tell you about what is going on in your community and where you can find help. Your local chamber of commerce, small business development group, and local economic development office are good resources for what is currently available in the community. They can tell you if there are current chamber members in your area connected with wellness. The small business development group and the economic development office can both inform you about what areas in your community need to be served. They may also have information about whether your community is overloaded with wellness organizations. In addition, the small business development group may have information regarding businesses that are closing (this is helpful if you are looking to buy or lease office space).

The United Way and the Salvation Army may be able to inform you about the needs of the underserved in your community. Your local community college and university are sources for education about specific areas where you may need additional training. They may also be able to let you know about wellness partnerships that already exist in your community. If your local hospital has a wellness center connected with it, you can learn about how your local medical community views wellness. The local department of tourism may be able to tell you whether your community is viewed as a wellness destination. Hotels would have information regarding how often people look for wellness activities. Your local YMCA can tell you what activities are well received and give you an idea of the wellness pulse for your area.

Another possible partnership would be with local celebrities. They may be willing to endorse your center. Or maybe you know someone who is nationally recognized. You could explore possible partnerships with people who are well known locally, regionally, or nationally to help market your center. If there are colleges or universities in your area, it may be possible to work with their athletic departments, business departments, information technology departments, or art departments to have their interns work with you for a semester (or more) to gain necessary experience. These can truly be win/win situations. Interns who work in your business may turn into full-time employees.

Most importantly, develop your own inner circle of support. The fire element is connected with the awakened heart. It is about partnerships. Partnerships are defined a little differently in the Five Element theory than in our American culture. Partnerships exist in a broader framework: owner/customer is a partnership; trainer/client is a partnership; teacher/student is another partnership. Through these partnerships, we deepen our connections, knowing that we are not in this alone. This reinforces our deep connection as human beings (Ornish 1998).

Hopefully, those in your inner circle of support are partnering with you to offer you a level of trust. Trust that you know you are supported in this endeavor. Trust that you can count on them to give you that needed boost. Trust that they discuss issues with an open mind and heart rather than from their own agenda. It is important that they maintain the attitude of speaking with your best interest at heart, which at times may be a challenge. At times, having to start those conversations may feel awkward, almost like learning how to ride a bike all over again. And even though it takes courage to have those challenging conversations, they are well worth the effort. You can gain clarity that will help you know where you stand and develop a clear vision of what you want for your center.

Chapter 7

Marketing Issues: Target Market

Marketing is about creating and maintaining relationships with your customers. You want people to know how they will benefit from your wellness center. Through effective marketing, you can promote your business uniquely to the public.

Most marketing decisions are based on addressing specific issues. You will want to look at who you want to bring into your business and how you want to present yourself. You may want to create some type of branding for your business, so that when people see a particular logo or hear a particular phrase, they connect it with your business. Then you need to look at how to market your business externally, including such things as pricing, customer service, and public relations. When you explore these issues, there is a greater likelihood for a successful business. You can break these down into the following categories: price, product, place, and promotion. This is often called the "marketing mix." Businesses that address each of these areas have greater success than those that focus on just business promotion.

The Marketing Mix

Price

Price, obviously, is what you charge for your services and products. How will you accept payment—cash or charge? Are you going to offer various membership plans and payment options? Will you offer discounts for multiple services (also called bundling)? Will you offer volume discounts? Will you offer different prices for different seasons of the year?

Product

Your products include the features and services you offer at your center. How will the services be offered—individually or matched up in packages? Your center's environment is a part of your product. What type of atmosphere do you want to present to clients as they enter your facility? How are you going to brand your facility and products? Your staff is another aspect of your product. It is important that prior to choosing employees, you decide what kind of people you will hire, not only in their education, certifications, and experiences but also in their philosophy; this will enable you to present the best product possible.

Place

The actual building where your center is located is part of this aspect, as is availability of parking. Is there parking on the premises or nearby, or will customers have to park on the street? Is the facility handicap accessible? Is it convenient to mass transportation? Are you going to sell products in addition to selling services? Is the location suitable for your type of business?

Promotion

Marketing is more than just advertising in newspapers, in magazines, and on the Internet. The best marketing provides a personal connection through activities such as community events, promotional celebrations, public speaking engagements, and of course word of mouth.

Part of marketing your wellness center involves educating the public. The better people understand your service, the more likely they are to use it. You could write articles for local magazines or newspapers, and attending local health fairs is another good way to promote your center.

The Internet is a crucial part of business in today's society. You will want to find a good designer to help create a website for your center. Pick a site that you like and contact their webmaster. Facebook, Twitter, and blogs are other venues that can help you promote your business.

After addressing the four parameters of price, product, place, and promotion, you are now ready to look at the people who will come to your center. You may already be very clear about the population that you want to serve. However, potential customers may need to be educated about the necessity of your service.

A good avenue to pursue is to create a focus group to examine where the participants' needs match your passion. Focus groups can help you get a clearer view of the target market you want to serve. Below is a short explanation of focus groups and target markets.

Focus Groups

A focus group is a marketing tool that provides qualitative research regarding your center. By bringing together a group of individuals who are interested in your service, you can gain information about your community and how they view wellness (Marczak and Sewell, n.d.). For example, you may want to create a focus group that explores what types of services people in your community want to have. Focus groups may even provide some creative new ideas about services they may want to add to your center.

There are many resources that show how to conduct a focus group. Managementhelp.org/evaluatn/focusgrp.htm and ag.arizona.edu/fcs/cyfernet/cyfar/focus.htm are easy-to-understand websites that give you clear information about focus groups.

Target Market

In the business classes that I taught massage students, they often stated that they wanted to work with all types of people. They said they were afraid to limit their practice. What I have found very interesting is that many of those students who initially believed that philosophy came back to visit years later as professionals and said they realized that they really should have targeted a specific market. They felt like their business was scattered. By trying to offer all services to all people, you often end up offering very little service to anyone. The clearer that you can be about the groups you want to serve, the better focus your business will have.

Your target market is the group of people you wish to serve and who have a need for your services. Target markets are defined by such characteristics as age, socioeconomic levels, ethnicity, marital status, education, hobbies/interests, home ownership, and levels of discretionary income, to name a few. By examining these factors, you can determine who your target market is and whether you can serve unmet needs.

When you have determined your target market, you can then create your niche. Some centers focus strictly on physical wellness; you may want to market your center as focusing on mental and spiritual wellness. Or you might create a center that appeals to the higher socio-economic demographic in your community. Could the community support a high-end center that includes all aspects of wellness: physical, emotional, mental, and spiritual? Maybe you are only interested in serving women. Some centers are marketed to families; they offer a range of activities that touch every age group. By finding a niche where there is a need, your center has a greater likelihood of success. You will have created a service that fills a need in the community, and the business will be less likely to have competition.

Marketing Plan

A key to business success is a solid marketing plan. Your marketing plan is a tool that helps to keep you focused. It is part of your internal planning. Your local small business development group may be able to assist you with your marketing plan. Many local community colleges offer marketing classes online so you can take them at your convenience. Local chambers of commerce often have monthly networking groups, which may be another source of useful information; you could even find someone to mentor you. And of course, the Internet has many resources for developing marketing plans as well as tutorials you can take in the comfort of your home.

You need to include several components in your marketing plan, starting with your overview or executive summary. You should include some analysis of the company. How does it stand ready for its market? You will want to have a situational assessment and analysis, which would outline your strengths, weaknesses, opportunities, and threats (SWOT). In the SWOT analysis, you would include an analysis of your competition. You would also want to have an analysis of the economic environment. Include the political environment, the economic and social environments, and the technology environment. You would also include some type of market analysis. This would include a marketing assessment and target market analysis. You will want to have an action plan with such elements as advertising, promotion, publicity, community relations, budget, and timetables. In simple terms, your marketing plan defines your business, your product/service, your competition, your customers, and your budget. Addressing these issues will give you a clearer picture of your process and your goals.

Chapter 8

Employees

Hiring people to work for you can be more complex than it seems. What types of positions will your center need? Do you want them to work as employees or can they be independent contractors? Would it serve the business to have people be consultants to the business? You may want to have some people on retainer, such as your lawyer, accountant, bookkeeper, and marketing person. Or you may want to partner with your local university and have interns work at your facility.

Again, it is certainly worthwhile to meet with a consultant to explore whether these positions could be filled by employees or independent contractors.

Whether you hire employees or have people work as independent contractors, it is critical for the high standards of your business that all employees have the required certifications and licensures that are required by your state. Please be sure to check into that area. You could pay thousands of dollars in penalties by hiring someone without the appropriate qualifications.

Hiring independent contractors may seem easier than hiring employees—less paperwork to fill out as well as not as much insurance for you to pay. However, there are very specific criteria used in determining whether someone can be an independent contractor. Let's explore this a little more.

Employees vs. Independent Contractors

When deciding whether to hire employees or independent contractors, there are some clear and simple questions to consider. The IRS Employer's Tax Guide, Publication 15-A, is available online at www.irs.gov/pub/irs-pdf/p15a.pdf and addresses factors that determine whether the people working for you are employees or independent contractors.

The first factor is behavior control: Do you decide when and where the person works? What tools or equipment are to be used—personal or owned by the company? What workers will be available to assist with the work? Who purchases supplies? What type of work is to be performed? Who determines in what order the work is to be performed? Has the employer offered training for this person (if yes, this person is probably an employee).

Financial control is another factor. Are expenses reimbursed? Expenses incurred by employees are usually reimbursed. Independent contractors may have a significant investment in the facilities used. Employees do not. Does the company put restrictions on where the person can work? Independent contractors have the freedom to seek other business opportunities in the area. Employees often are restricted. How are they paid? This is a key factor in the decision. Independent contractors are paid a flat fee and are not paid commission. Taxes are not taken out, and worker's compensation is not covered by the employer. Independent contractors have the ability to make a profit or a loss.

The type of relationship is the final factor. Do you pay the person benefits? If you offer health insurance, vacation or sick pay, or a pension plan, that person is considered an employee. The length of term of the relationship is also considered under this factor. If you intend to have the person work for an extended period of time, it is better to consider them an employee. The final aspect of this factor is how key they are to the workings of the company. If you are looking for someone to be a personal trainer or a massage therapist for your center, it is best to have them as an employee. To view this information in complete detail, you can go to the IRS site to view the publication listed above.

When you decide that you are going to have employees, you must get a federal employer identification number (EIN), which you can apply for online at https://sa1.www4.irs.gov/modiein/individual/index.jsp. You will also need to apply for a state EIN as well. Check with your state. Your local small business development group can discuss any other requirements.

What kind of practitioners are you going to have in your center? You should only hire people who have appropriate certification/licensure to perform the discipline you are requesting. Be sure to check with your state's regulatory body for each of the disciplines that your center provides. You should be able to go to the department of licensing and regulation to get that information. In addition to finding out any specific licensure requirements, you will also want to verify each applicant's licensing/certification. Most state licensing boards provide lists of licensed individuals. Be sure to require copies of all licenses and certifications that an applicant claims to possess. Finally, be sure to obtain and check out appropriate references for potential employees. Look for professional references instead of personal references. If all of an applicant's references are family members or friends, this may be a red flag.

Some businesses also require a background check. Your local police department may be able to help with this.

Earth

Earth Element

Buildings, too, are children of the earth and sun.
—Frank Lloyd Wright.

Earth element is expressed in the season that Five Element theory refers to as late summer. It occurs in late August. The function of this season is to show gratitude for life, to live from a sense of abundance, and to nourish all by thoughtful tending and simple gifts. Here is where we offer our service. It is our center. So here is our physical center. From here we examine what we want our center to look like.

The bounty is shared and goods are delivered. From here we know when to offer what is needed in the moment. This season demonstrates transformation, completion, thoughtfulness, and service (Balles 2004).

From here we nurture life on all levels. We take in the raw material and transform it into something useful. Eventually this becomes our harvest. The late summer embodies the virtues of gratitude, appreciation, and integration (Balles 2004).

In this section, you will dream about what you want your center to be. You will explore the ideas of the physical space, the people working in your center, the atmosphere that radiates from your center, and your goal for the space and the people who come to the space. Your center is the physical center of your work and an expression of something larger. Can you actually imagine yourself there? What will it look like? How will it feel?

Chapter 9

What Type of Center?

If you create a needs assessment for your community at large and for specific groups, you can learn how your center can serve the community (although some people follow the concept of "build it and they will come"). A key question is, for whose sake are you building this center? What are their demographics—their age, income, and so forth? These issues were addressed in the marketing chapter and certainly influence what type of center you will open.

The physical space makes an unconscious impression on us. One means of creating your interior design is to use feng shui. This is the ancient art of placement. According to Hope Karan Gerecht (1999), feng shui is both a science and an art. You can also say it is the Chinese way of interior design. The purpose of feng shui is to balance your immediate environment to promote harmony, happiness, and success. In addition to analyzing your immediate physical surroundings, a feng shui consultant will explore information about you as the owner, using the Five Element theory, so that you are well positioned to make changes to raise the energy of the business to a higher degree (Gerecht 1999).

Feng shui is a method of relating or connecting your physical surroundings with specific aspects of life. The road map used is called *ba-gua, pa-kua,* or the nine palaces. The specific areas of consideration in the nine palaces are career, knowledge, family, prosperity, recognition, marriage/partnership, children/creativity, helpful people/travel, and health. Color, shape, light, placement, and the elements are some of the tools used in balancing your environment. An example of working with feng shui would be to examine your building's entrance to ensure that the space is open and welcoming. If by chance there is a wall that blocks the flow of the energy, feng shui can offer tools to help the flow. These tools are used to create the best environment for improved health, increased business and career advancement, support in creating closer relationships, increased spirituality, deepened wisdom, and ultimately feelings of greater joy and happiness in any structure, whether residential or commercial (Gerecht 1999).

In today's world, you should think about your carbon footprint. Can you incorporate "green" into your center? Do you want to start by building a green facility? Are you interested in what impact your facility will have on the environment, the economy, and the society? What measures will you use to reduce energy consumption? Can you design natural light into the facility to supplement the artificial lighting? How can you address the issue of water consumption in your facility? You should attempt to use recycled materials whenever possible.

When exploring what type of center you want to create, there are a number of issues to be addressed. These include how broad or narrow your focus will be. Do you want to draw clients for general wellness or do you want to focus on people who want to address a specific portion of wellness such as weight training? Keep in mind; it is always beneficial to partner with people who are already in this field. They may be an invaluable resource for your center. Listed below are a number of different types of wellness centers and some websites that can help you decide if they are right for you.

Fitness

If you choose to open a fitness center, you can focus on a very specific target group, such as people who are interested in body building or strict weight training, or you may want to include the broader cardio and strength training or maybe cardio rehab and cancer rehab.

Will your center offer a broad array of services such as individual training with the options of having personal trainers, group classes with instructors, and workshops? Will your center also focus on other aspects of wellness, including spiritual, mental, and emotional sides of wellness in addition to physical wellness?

Below is a list of associations that address fitness. They include training, certification, continuing education, and much more. Their mission statements have been included for you.

The American College of Sports Medicine promotes and integrates scientific research, education, and the practical application of sports medicine and exercise to maintain and enhance physical performance, fitness, health, and quality of life. (www.acsm.org/AM/Template.cfm?Section=About_ACSM)

The American Aerobics Association/International Sport Medicine Association is a "full spectrum certification association" that certifies instructors and trainers in primary and step aerobics, holistic health, personal fitness, weight training, and fitness. (www.aaai-ismafitness.com)

The American Council on Exercise (ACE) is a nonprofit organization committed to enriching the quality of life through safe and effective physical activity. As an authority on fitness, ACE protects all segments of society against ineffective fitness products, programs, and trends through its ongoing public education, outreach, and research. ACE further protects the public by setting certification and continuing education standards for fitness professionals. (www.acefitness.org)

You can get information on the most popular equipment used in fitness centers at the following websites:

- www.nautilus.com
- www.startrac.com
- www.precor.com
- www.lifefitness.com

The Spa Trade Association offers a listing of associations for spas and medical spas. (www.spatrade.com/resources/index.phtml?act=associations)

In their book *The Spirit and Science of Holistic Health,* Robison and Carrier (2004) include a chapter on designing a holistic program. They have taken traditional biomedical health program concepts and offer specific suggestions that make some of those traditional ideas more suitable for a holistic center. The following excerpts are offered with permission from the authors:

Life center (instead of fitness facility): For those that have one, the physical facility is often the most visible symbol of the program. It is therefore very important to "soften" the facility. Move away from strict emphasis on physical health, cardio-vascular condition, and strength training. It is also helpful to create resource and support areas throughout the facility that encourage relaxation and socialization and that help people explore a broad range of health and life issues. (Robison and Carrier 2004, 304)

Life center staff (instead of professional trainers and aerobic instructors): Wellness programs are traditionally staffed by biomedically trained, middle class, thin, young, white, stereotypically fit-looking people. Wellness program participants, however, often represent a wide spectrum of ages, economic status, races, religions, body sizes, and fitness levels. For holistic health promotion programs, it is important to create a more diverse staff that can effectively and compassionately relate to the needs of many types of people. (Robison and Carrier 2004, 305)

Robison and Carrier further develop these concepts by focusing on such concepts as life simplification (rather than stress management), creating a life balance questionnaire (rather than a health risk appraisal), and developing wellness extravaganzas (instead of health fairs). They also discuss eliminating such practices as fitness evaluations, exercise prescriptions, and incentive programs. The holistic health promotion model creates a place that is inclusive rather than exclusive in all aspects of the center. Their book is an excellent resource for any wellness facility.

Medical Spa

Medical spas are becoming very popular. They offer clients the opportunity for both medical treatment and alternative self-care under one roof. Medical spas may offer services from physicians, chiropractors, Ayurvedic doctors, acupuncturists, herbal medicine practitioners, massage therapists, estheticians, life/wellness coaches, counselors, dietitians, yoga instructors, spiritual leaders, cosmetologists, dermatologists, cosmetic surgeons, naturopathic doctors, hypnotherapists, fitness trainers, and others. The key to a medical spa is that it is run by a licensed health care professional.

Below are two associations with their mission statements:

The International Medical Spa Association: A medical spa is a facility that operates under the full-time supervision of a licensed health care professional. The facility operates within the scope of practice of its staff and offers traditional, complementary, and alternative heath care practices and treatments in a spa-like setting. Practitioners working in a medical spa will be governed by their appropriate licensing board, if licensing is required. The definition is used widely in the industry. (www.medicalspaassociation.org/index.asp)

The Medical Spa Society: It is the mission of our society of professional spa and medical practitioners to promote education, communication, and standards of excellence for the medical spa profession. We are committed to providing educational forums that allow our industry to stay informed about the latest innovations and cutting-edge developments in the spa and medical fields. We offer many rich resources, which will promote strategic planning that will help grow our businesses. Our society is dedicated to the advancement of the medical spa industry in all respects, including the interests of members, their staff, and the consumer. Our goal is to encourage the exchange of information and ideas, and to develop and to adhere to high standards of care and a code of ethics. This will enhance the image and credibility of the entire medical spa industry. (www.medicalspasociety.com)

Spa

Spas are emerging in all sorts of communities. The number of spas in the United States increased by 18.8 percent to 21,300 between 2007 and 2008, according to the International SPA Association 2009 U.S. Spa Industry Update. They offer a wide range of therapies, depending on the setting, including service from physicians, chiropractors, Ayurvedic doctors, massage therapists, estheticians, life/wellness coaches, counselors, dietitians, yoga instructors, spiritual leaders, cosmetologists, dermatologists, cosmetic surgeons, naturopathic doctors, hypnotherapists, fitness trainers, and others (Williams 2007).

Treatments range from paraffin dips to body wraps, various types of hydrotherapy, aromatherapy, bodywork, foot treatments, fangotherapy (mud treatments), and thalassotherapy (use of marine environments and sea products) (Williams 2007).

The following organizations offer education and information on spas:

The American Spa Therapies Education and Certification Council offers postgraduate education in a variety of spa therapy curricula, including spa management. (www.astecc.com)

The Day Spa Association offers information regarding spa etiquette (for example, how the therapist should greet the client) and the ambiance of the spa. This association also lists guidelines of what customers should expect to receive when visiting a member of the association. (www. dayspaassociation.com)

Integrative Medicine

Integrative medicine, as defined by the American Association of Integrative Medicine, is a dynamic alliance combining approaches to health care. The alliance includes the practice of conventional, natural, alternative, complementary, and herbal remedies. This approach is often referred to as holistic medicine or alternative medicine.

Many of the professionals listed in the spa section can also be considered if you are opening an integrative medicine center. Some areas to consider in an integrative medicine center: How much of the service do you want to offer at your center, and how much do you want to out source? Would it be better to partner with professionals in the community or to have professionals right in the center?

The National Center for Complementary and Alternative Medicine, which is part of the National Institutes of Health, is a great resource for you. (nccam.nih.gov)

Two other associations for integrative medicine are the American Association of Integrative Medicine (www.aaimedicine.com) and the Association of Integrative Medicine. (www.integrativemedicine.org/index.html)

No matter what type of center you want to open, you want it to be a place for healing. Healing is a process of recovery, repair, and return to wholeness, according to Wayne Jonas (2006) in the Samueli Institute's *Optimal Healing Environments* (OHE) brochure. There are many factors that enter into creating healing environments. The chart below outlines the components for optimal healing environments as developed at the Samueli Institute by Ronald Chez, Kenneth Pelletier, and Wayne Jonas for the Second American Samueli Symposium. These seven major areas have been determined to create optimal healing in health care environments. These are easily transferable to a center whose focus is wellness and healing.

According to Jonas and Chez (2004), the optimal healing environment is one in which the social, psychological, spiritual, physical, and behavioral components of health care are oriented toward support and stimulation of healing and the achievement of wholeness. In our opinion, these components include:

1. Conscious development of intention, awareness, expectation, and belief in improvement and well-being;
2. Transformative self-care practices that facilitate personal integration and the experience of wholeness and well-being;
3. Techniques that foster a palpable healing presence based on compassion, love, and awareness of interconnectivity;
4. Development of listening and communication skills that foster trust and a bond, sometimes called the therapeutic alliance, between practitioner and patient;
5. Instruction and practice in health promotion behaviors that change lifestyle to support self-healing and the development of social support and service;
6. Responsible application of integrative medicine via the collaborative application of conventional and complementary practices in a manner supportive of healing processes;
7. The physical space in which healing is practiced, including characteristics of light, music, architecture, and color among other elements that can influence the impact on an OHE. (Jonas and Chez 2004, S-1)

The chart and its various components are included in this chapter for your information and use. The chart was reprinted with permission of the Samueli Institute.

OPTIMAL HEALING ENVIRONMENTS

SAMUELI INSTITUTE
EXPLORING THE SCIENCE OF HEALING
WWW.SAMUELIINSTITUTE.ORG

INNER ENVIRONMENT

Developing Healing Beliefs *(ENHANCE AWARENESS)*
- Expectation
- Hope
- Understanding
- Intention

Experiencing Personal Wholeness *(ENHANCE INTEGRATION)*
- Self-Care
- Mind
- Body
- Spirit
- Energy

Cultivating Healing Relationships *(ENHANCE CARING)*
- Compassion
- Empathy
- Social Support
- Communication
- Family Involvement

OUTER ENVIRONMENT

Practicing Healthy Lifestyles *(ENHANCE HEALTH HABITS)*
- Diet
- Exercise
- Relaxation
- Balance

Applying Integrative Health Care *(ENHANCE MEDICAL CARE)*
- Conventional Medicine
- Complementary Practices
- Ethno-Cultural Traditions

Creating Healing Organizations *(ENHANCE PROCESS & STRUCTURE)*
- Leadership
- Mission
- Finance
- Workforce
- Technology
- Evaluation
- Service

Building Healing Spaces *(ENHANCE SENSORY INPUT)*
- Nature
- Color
- Light
- Positive Distraction
- Architecture
- Aroma
- Music
- Green

金

Metal

Metal Element

Metal creates a mysterious point of consolidated matter,
where a continuous in-breath and out-breath merge together.
—David M. Bell

The metal element is the gift of the season of autumn. In this season, we acknowledge things as they are and let go. From here we acknowledge respect, both giving and receiving it. We let go of what does not serve any longer. It is our quality control. We explore what has merit—what stays and what goes.

From here we honor the true giftedness of all beings. We acknowledge the uniqueness of all aspects of creation. From this season we are inspired and revitalized, while retaining our special quality and purity. The metal element of the autumn embodies honor, respect, reverence, and inspiration (Balles 2004).

From this season we also show how well we can let go of what no longer serves us. When we do that, we then create a space for something new to enter. In this season is demonstrated the necessity letting go and leaving behind, which are the beginnings of changes (Balles 2004).

In this section, you will learn about legal issues that can help your center take shape. The policies and the procedures for the center also add to the shape and form of your center. Here we will examine what aspects will stay and what will go. The nuts and bolts of the actual location of the center and the day-to-day operations help determine what has merit. These are also aspects of your quality control.

Chapter 10

Legal Issues

In starting any business, you need to know what is required in your local, state, and federal regulations. At the federal level, the Small Business Administration (www.sba.gov) is a great resource for new businesses. A good resource at the state level is your secretary of state or your consumer affairs office. At the local level, check with your city hall or county planning and zoning committees. Many states also have a department of licensing and regulations that can assist you. Your local small business development group is always a great place for partnerships.

A Dun & Bradstreet number is required for businesses interested in applying for grants. You can apply online at www.dnb.com/us/duns_update/index.html.

Licenses/Permits/Zoning

Contact your licensing bureau to find out what is needed to start your particular business. What permits does your state/county/city require? Most areas require a license to operate.

To protect the community, many cities and counties have zoning laws. Properties may be zoned for residential, business, industrial, or agricultural use, to name a few. Remember to check for any local neighborhood community associations. When looking for a location, research whether the building is zoned for your type of business. Be sure to check the exact location. In some areas, zoning changes from lot to lot or from building to building.

What does your local health department require? Health departments often require some type of license to operate. Be sure to inquire there.

If you are going to sell products, you will be required to obtain a license allowing you to collect sales tax. The State Department of Revenue should be able to assist you with that step.

In looking for a location, you will want to check with your local jurisdiction for their requirements. They may have requirements about how much off-street parking must be available, how many bathrooms you must have, and other considerations unique to your locality. There are federal requirements (the Americans with Disabilities Act, or ADA) for ensuring that buildings are accessible for disabled people. You will want to check this website for information: www.ADA.gov/publicat. htm#Anchor-ADA-44867.

Once you have decided on the location, if there are changes to be made to the building, you will need building permits. This requirement makes sure that the building conforms to the county building and safety codes. You will also want to check with the fire department for fire safety. You may be required to have fire inspection certificates posted somewhere. Then when everything is completed, inspected, and ready to go, you will receive an occupancy permit.

Taxes

The tax laws can be complicated and confusing. It is in your best interest and in the best interest of your business to contact a tax lawyer, to ensure that you are in compliance with the law. The IRS has a thorough website with tax information (www.irs.gov/businesses/index. html). It lists the various taxes that are required such as federal income tax, Social Security and Medicare taxes, federal unemployment tax, self-employment tax (if you are a sole proprietorship), and depositing employment tax, to name a few. Taxes must be filed quarterly. Again, check with the IRS and your local small business administration for requirements and assistance.

HIPAA Considerations

Regarding confidentiality, if you are going to be working with any third-party reimbursement or if you are sending any patient information across the Internet or by fax, you are required to have all patients complete specific paperwork pertaining to privacy of medical records, and you are required to maintain records in a specific format. It definitely is to your advantage to get advice and support to make sure you are in compliance under the HIPAA. HIPAA stands for Health Insurance Portability and Accountability Act of 1996 (HIPAA). If this term is new to you, I recommend that you look at www.hhs.gov/ocr/privacy/index.html. This act covers the privacy of health information and the rights of individuals regarding their health information. The website offers a good deal of information and training for you if your business is regulated under HIPAA.

Insurance

This is a very important spoke in the legal wheel. You should talk with an insurance agent. You will need liability insurance that covers business-related injuries to visitors to your property. (This coverage may not be included in your lease.) It does not cover any employees or you.

Small business insurance provides umbrella coverage for business losses, interruption of your business, problems with any products you might have sold, any other errors or omissions that may have occurred, and any issues of general liability.

Malpractice liability insurance protects you if a client claims losses incurred due to you or an employee acting negligently or failing to perform at a professional level.

You will also want to have fire and theft insurance that protects your equipment, furniture, products, and records. If you are renting space, this is sometimes called renter's insurance.

There are other protective options, such as business interruption insurance, personal disability insurance, medical health insurance, product liability insurance (if you will sell products), and worker's compensation (if you have employees).

Consult with an agent to be sure you are adequately covered.

Employer Requirements

As stated in the section on employees, you must have both a federal and a state EIN. The federal form is SS-4. For the state form, you will need to check with your particular state agency. Your employees must complete a Form I-9, Employment Eligibility Verification (from the US Department of Justice, Immigration and Naturalization Service). They are also required to complete a W-4 Employee's Withholding Allowance Certification. For state withholdings, check with your state employment department for requirements.

Chapter 11

Nuts and Bolts

Things to Consider

Have you decided whether you want to rent or buy? Renting can be nice because you pay one monthly amount, and the landlord takes care of the rest. Confirm what is included in the rental price such as utilities, heat, water, sewage, and trash pickup. If you are renting, what kinds of changes can you make to the space? Who will incur those expenses? If you incur those expenses, will there be a reduction in the rent?

If you buy, in addition to the purchase price, you may have to incur renovation costs. If you renovate, will the combined total of the purchase price and the renovation costs make it difficult to recoup your investment if you sell the space at a later time? Is it worth renovating? Or is it more effective to purchase land and build a new facility?

Whether you are renting or buying, consider the heating system. How old is it? Does it meet current standards or codes? How large is the system's carbon footprint? Is it noisy when it comes on or goes off? (You do not want a noisy heater if your wellness center programs offer relaxation techniques.) What is the electrical panel's load capacity? Will it be able to handle the requirements of the equipment you intend to use, or does it need to be upgraded?

How many square feet do you require? How many treatment rooms will you need? How much space is needed for equipment? How much space will you require for storage? What kind of bathroom facilities will you need? Is the plumbing adequate to carry the load required? Do you need to have locker rooms? Will clients need access to showers? Is the space adequate enough for handicap accessibility? Is the space adequate for larger people to use?

Do you want to have kitchen facilities? What is the space like for staff? Is there space to hold washers and dryers? Those considerations often get pushed by the wayside.

Location, Location, Location!

The location of your center can make all the difference in its success or failure. Does the building have curb appeal? Would people want to come there? Is it handicap accessible? To verify ADA compliance, you can go to www.ADA.gov/publicat.htm#Anchor-ADA-44867.

Again, what are the jurisdictional considerations? Is the property zoned for the type of business you want to put there? Will you need to go to your local planning and zoning to request an exemption? Is there easy access and adequate parking?

Here are some additional issues you may want to consider: Is the facility close to a school, fire department, or police station? (There may be noise and traffic issues.) Is the business near a busy interstate? That may seem like a positive factor. However, if it is too close to the highway, as clients attempt to relax, they may be disturbed by noise from the big rigs, which may make relaxing more difficult. All of those considerations have an impact on your business.

Business Plan

Developing a good business plan is crucial in the creation of a successful business. It becomes a roadmap to follow. A good business plan will help you set out a clear vision. It will help you evaluate the market and calculate your costs, allowing you to forecast the business's growth while at the same time helping you determine the level of risk you may be undertaking. A business plan is necessary if you are going to approach a bank for funding.

Many components are necessary when creating a good business plan. However, the way that you format your business plan depends on your audience as well as the complexity of your business. Your business plan obviously needs a cover page and a table of contents. Next you will want to have statement of your purpose and an executive summary. Then you move into the section where you talk about the business, which includes the business description, operating procedures, and personnel. The next sections should discuss your marketing components, competition assessment, and risk analysis. Of course, you must include a section on financial data. Here you will address your current financial status, your forecast for your financial future, your costs, and your potential income. You will also want to address capital equipment and supplies. Finally, you will want to include a section with supporting documents. This section would include, but is not limited to, operating balance sheets, business income and expense forecasts, monthly business and personal budget worksheets, and information on cash flow. Also include tax forms for the past three years, copies of leases, legal agreements, resumes of all principal members, letters of intent from suppliers, and copies of all necessary licenses and legal documents.

There are a variety of ways to create a good business plan. If this seems like a daunting task, you do have options. On-line courses are available through the federal government and your local community college. Many community colleges also offer courses on starting up businesses and writing business plans as well as marketing plans.

There are many great resources on the Internet for information on writing a business plan, including www.sba.gov/smallbusinessplanner/plan/writeabusinessplan/index.html and www.businessmastery.us/supplements/biz-plan.php.

Creating a good business plan can be a long process, but it is well worth the effort.

Chapter 12

Policies and Procedures for the Center

When creating any type of business, it is prudent to have policies and procedures in place. You can develop a single policies and procedures manual, or you can set up two separate manuals.

The policy manual is based on your company's philosophy; it is its foundation. Therefore, start with your vision and mission statements and include your purpose, priorities, and goals. At the top of the list include customer relations, such as your cancellation policy, your policy for staff interaction with the clients, and your expectations of clients. If your cancellation policy is inadequate, it could cost your business a great deal of money in lost revenue.

This manual should do more than just describe the qualifications of personnel. It should also describe the requirements and expectations of staff members. You can include chain of command, scheduling, and salary information. This includes pay periods, timing of pay increases, bonuses, vacation and sick leave, tardiness, benefit packages, and overtime. Your policies manual should also include dress codes, hygiene, drug testing, smoking on premises, phone use, and discounts available for employees. It is imperative to include evaluations, types of disciplinary actions, and dismissal/termination procedures. Include steps employees must take to submit a grievance against another employee or the owners.

The procedures portion of the manual covers how the business operates on a day-to-day basis. This information includes details about what your front desk staff needs to do to start each day. By looking at the procedures manual, employees would know step by step the company's policies and procedures for telephone etiquette, scheduling and rescheduling appointments, and handling payments. They could find what paperwork is needed for new clients to complete. Also include the financial arrangements, as well as how to close out the money at the end of each day. The procedures would explain how to write up sales, how to maintain the equipment, and what should be done in the event of an emergency.

All clients should fill out an intake form. This form gives their medical history. Fitness centers may substitute an intake form with a physical activity readiness questionnaire. Informed consent forms indicate that clients understand what will be happening during their session. This form is necessary, particularly when working with clients receiving any type of integrative medicine modality. Forms should be created with clients' rights and responsibilities in mind.

Chapter 13

The Beginning

Now you have a place from which to start! My goal was to offer some pointers about where to begin to explore this great adventure. This book's appendix gives a sample of some forms that you will need at your center. The forms are also available on-line at www.businessnation.com/library/forms, www.irs.gov/businesses/small/article/0,,id=99200,00.html, and www.businessmastery.us/forms.php.

Wellness is a passion of mine, and if you are looking to create a wellness center, it is certainly a passion of yours. To create your center, envision it and declare it into existence. Remember to refer back to the Five Elements. Each element is not only part of a season, it is part of you. The water element is your potency and power, your courage. It is within you. In the wood element, you possess the ability to strategize and plan. From here you look at all sides of an issue and then get things done. Your exploration of partnerships comes through the fire element. From here you demonstrate insight, responsibility, compassion, and understanding. In the element of earth, which is your center, comes your ability to show gratitude and to live from a sense of abundance. And finally, through the metal element, we acknowledge respect and the uniqueness of all aspects of creation. From here we let go of that which no longer serves, so we have space for something new to enter.

Play and have fun! Just imagine, as a client walks up to the center, what do you want them to see—plants, colors, and sounds? What draws a client into the center? Are the colors inviting? Do they create a positive invitation? Does the architecture flow? Can the client move freely and easily from one area to another while feeling safe and welcomed? Do the aromas and music enhance their visit? And how does the center help serve the environment? Is the space environmentally friendly? Use your imagination to create a wellness center that expresses your hopes and dreams for you and for your community.

May this process be a journey of great discovery and service to the world.

Bibliography

Balles, T. 2004. *Dancing with ten thousand things*. Lincoln, NE: iUniverse.

Bell, D. M. 2004. *Spirit of nature—The harmony of the Five Elements: A path to healing.* South Melbourne: Lothian Books.

Gerecht, H. K. 1999. *Healing design*. Boston: Journey Editions.

Hay, L. L. 1987. *You can heal your life*. Carson: Hay House.

Idel, E., and Kasl, S. 1991. Health perceptions and survival: Do global evaluations of health status really predict mortality? *Journal of Gerontology 46*(2), 555–65.

Illich, I. 1976. *Limits to medicine, medical nemesis: The expropriation of health.* New York: Penguin.

Jonas, W., and Chez, R. A. 2004. Toward optimal healing environments in healthcare. *Journal of Alternative and Complementary Medicine. 10*(1), S-1–S-6.

Morris, D. 2007. *Illness and culture in the post modern age.* Berkeley: University of California Press.

Ornish, D. 1998. *Love and survival: The scientific basis for the healing power of intimacy.* New York: HarperCollins.

Robison, J. 2003. Holistic health promotion workshop. Rocky Gap State Park, Flintstone, MD.

Robison, J., and Carrier, K. 2004. *The spirit and science of holistic health.* Bloomington, IN: AuthorHouse.

Seaward, B. 2001. *Health of the human spirit, spiritual dimension for personal health.* Needham Heights, MA: Allyn & Bacon.

Smith, C. E. 2006. *Awakening wisdom.* Siler City, NC: South Wind Press.

Sohnen-Moe, C. M. 2008. *Business mastery, 4th ed.* Tucson, AZ: Sohnen-Moe Associates.

Weil, A. 2009. *Self-Healing Newsletter.* Watertown, MA.

Williams, A. 2007. *Spa bodywork: A guide for massage therapists.* Baltimore: Lippincott Williams & Wilkins.

Websites

American Aerobics Association/International Sport Medicine Association. N.d. Home page. Retrieved January 22, 2011, from www.aaai-ismafitness.com

American Association of Integrative Medicine. 2011. Home page. Retrieved January 22, 2011, from www.aaimedicine.com

American College of Sports Medicine. 2007. Home page. Retrieved January 22, 2011, from www.acsm.org/AM/Template.cfm?Section=About_ACSM

American Council on Exercise. 2011. Home page. Retrieved January 22, 2011, from www.acefitness.org

American Spa Therapies Education and Certification Council. N.d. Home page. Retrieved January 22, 2011, from www.astecc.com

Association of Integrative Medicine. 2008. Home page. Retrieved January 22, 2011, from www.integrativemedicine.org/index.html

Business.Gov. 2011. Home page. Retrieved January 22, 2011, from www.business.gov

Cherie Sohnen-Moe Associates. Inc. 2011. *Reproducible forms, free office forms.* Retrieved January 22, 2011, www.businessmastery.us

Day Spa Association. 2000. Home page. Retrieved January 22, 2011, from www.dayspaassociation.com

Department of Agriculture. 2011. Retrieved January 22, 2011, from www.rurdev.usda.gov.

Department of Commerce, Census Bureau. 2010. *State and county quickfacts*. Retrieved January 22, 2011, from quickfacts.census.gov/qfd/states/24/24001.html

Department of Health and Human Services. N.d. *Health information privacy*. Retrieved January 22, 2011, from www.hhs.gov/ocr/privacy/index.html

Department of Justice. 2010. *ADA regulations and technical assistance materials*. Retrieved January 22, 2011, from www.ADA.gov/publicat.htm#Anchor-ADA-44867

Dun and Bradstreet. 2010. *D&B Duns number*. Retrieved January 22, 2011, from www.dnb.com/us/duns_update/index.html

Free Management Library. 2006. *Basics of conducting a focus group*. Retrieved January 22, 2011, from managementhelp.org/evaluatn/focusgrp.htm

Free Management Library. 2006. *Comparison between for-profit and nonprofit corporations*. Retrieved January 22, 2011, from managementhelp.org/boards/boards.htm#anchor98036

Internal Revenue Service. 2009. *EIN assistant*. Retrieved January 22, 2011, from https://www.irs.gov/modiein/individual/index.jsp.

Internal Revenue Service. 2011. *Employer's supplemental tax guide*. Retrieved January 22, 2011, from www.irs.gov/pub/irs-pdf/p15a.pdf

Internal Revenue Service. 2010. *Tax information for businesses*. Retrieved January 22, 2011, from www.irs.gov/businesses/index.html

International Medical Spa Association. 2011. Home page. Retrieved January 22, 2011, from www.medicalspaassociation.org/index.asp

Life Fitness. 2010. Home page. Retrieved January 22, 2011, from www.lifefitness.com

Marczak, M. and Sewell, M. N.d. *Using focus groups for evaluation*. Retrieved January 22, 2011, from ag.arizona.edu/sfcs/cyfernet/cyfar/focus.htm

Maryland Nonprofits. 2010. Home page. Retrieved January 22, 2011, from www.marylandnonprofits.org/

Maryland Office of the Secretary of State. 2003. *Checklist for starting a nonprofit organization in Maryland.* Retrieved January 22, 2011, from www.sos.state.md.us/Charity/ChecklistNonProfit.pdf

Medical Spa Society. 2007-2011. Home page. Retrieved January 22, 2011, from www.medicalspasociety.com

National Institutes of Health, National Center for Complementary and Alternative Medicine. 2011. Home page. Retrieved January 22, 2011, from nccam.nih.gov

Nautilus. 2011. Home page. Retrieved January 22, 2011, from www.nautilus.com

Precor. 2010. Home page. Retrieved January 22, 2011, from www.precor.com

Samueli Institute. 2006–2007. *Optimal Healing Environments.* Retrieved January 22, 2011, from www.samueliinstitute.org/research/research-home/optimal-healing.html

Small Business Administration. 2010. Home page. Retrieved January 22, 2011, from www.sba.gov

Small Business Administration. 2010. *Write a business plan.* Retrieved January 22, 2011, from www.sba.gov/smallbusinessplanner/plan/writeabusinessplan/index.html

Spa Trade. 2011. *Industry Associations.* Retrieved January 22, 2011, from www.spatrade.com/resources/index.phtml?act=associations

Startrac. 2011. Home page. Retrieved January 22, 2011, from www.startrac.com/welcome

Appendix
Business Start-Up Forms

Strategic Planning

Today's Date: _____ Target Date: _____ Date Achieved: _____

Purpose: _____

_____

_____

Priority: _____

_____

_____

Situation Description: _____

_____

_____

_____

Objective: _____

❑ Capitalize on this strength ❑ Change this condition ❑ Other _____

Goal: _____

_____

_____

Benefits of Achieving This Goal: _____

_____

_____

Possible Courses of Action:

1. _____

_____

2. _____

_____

3. _____

_____

4. _____

_____

Best Course of Action: _____

_____

_____

_____

Proposal Outline:

1. _____
   _____
2. _____
   _____
3. _____
   _____
4. _____
   _____

Advantages:

_____
_____
_____

Potential Conflicts/Disadvantages:	Solutions:
1. _____	1. _____
2. _____	2. _____
3. _____	3. _____
4. _____	4. _____
5. _____	5. _____
6. _____	6. _____

Action Required To Begin:

_____
_____
_____
_____
_____

Resources Needed:

_____
_____
_____
_____

	Specific Steps To Achieve This Goal	Target Date	Person Responsible
1.	_____	_____	_____
2.	_____	_____	_____
3.	_____	_____	_____
4.	_____	_____	_____
5.	_____	_____	_____
6.	_____	_____	_____
7.	_____	_____	_____
8.	_____	_____	_____
9.	_____	_____	_____
10.	_____	_____	_____
11.	_____	_____	_____
12.	_____	_____	_____
13.	_____	_____	_____
14.	_____	_____	_____
15.	_____	_____	_____
16.	_____	_____	_____
17.	_____	_____	_____
18.	_____	_____	_____
19.	_____	_____	_____
20.	_____	_____	_____
21.	_____	_____	_____
22.	_____	_____	_____
23.	_____	_____	_____
24.	_____	_____	_____
25.	_____	_____	_____

Procedure Manual Checklist

Overview
- ❑ Mission Statement.
- ❑ Summary of Company's Purpose, Priorities and Goals.
- ❑ Code of Ethics.
- ❑ Scope of Practice Statement.
- ❑ Standards of Practice Statement.

Business Management
- ❑ Confidentiality.
- ❑ HIPAA Guidelines and Forms.
- ❑ New Client Protocol.
- ❑ Fee Structure (Session, Packages, Sliding Fee, Free).
- ❑ Tipping.
- ❑ Payment Terms Available (Types, Insurance).
- ❑ Credit Card Acceptance (if so, which ones).
- ❑ Filing Insurance Forms.
- ❑ Safety Measures: OSHA requirements; Risk management; What to do in case of an emergency.
- ❑ Security.
- ❑ Care and Operation of Equipment.
- ❑ Cleaning and Maintenance.
- ❑ Hours of Operation.
- ❑ Procedures for Opening and Closing the Office.
- ❑ Desired Manner for Carrying out Routine Business Activities.
- ❑ Bookkeeping Instructions.

Staffing
- ❑ Qualifications: general personality requirements, educational standards, work history.
- ❑ Job Descriptions.
- ❑ Chain of Command.
- ❑ Work Hours and Scheduling.
- ❑ Finances: salary, raises, overtime, pay day, leaves of absence, tardiness, sick leave, bonuses, benefits package, reviews.
- ❑ Continuing Education (requirements, what the company will pay for).
- ❑ Evaluations.
- ❑ Personnel Records.
- ❑ Grievance Procedures.
- ❑ Phone Use.
- ❑ Dress Code.
- ❑ Hygiene & Scent.
- ❑ Smoking.
- ❑ Parking.
- ❑ Employee Purchasing Procedures and Discounts (of services and products).
- ❑ Actions Requiring Discipline and Specific Consequences.
- ❑ Disciplinary Procedures.
- ❑ Grounds for Termination.
- ❑ Communications with Allied Health Practitioners.
- ❑ Competition.
- ❑ Customer Relations: how clients are to be greeted, the forms they need to fill out, financial arrangements, rescheduling, dispensing educational materials.

Business Management
Forms

Balance Sheet

Balance Sheet as of _____

Assets

Current Assets
    Cash/Bank Balance $
    Accounts Receivable $
    Inventory $
    Supplies $

Fixed Assets
    Property $
    Equipment $

Total Assets $

Liabilities

Current Liabilities
    Accounts Payable $
    Credit Card Charges $

Long-Term Liabilities
    Bank Loans $

Total Liabilities $

Net Worth (Owner's Equity) $

Monthly Business Expense Worksheet

Expense	Estimated Monthly Cost	x 12
Rent	$ _____	$ _____
Utilities	$ _____	$ _____
Telephone	$ _____	$ _____
Bank Fees	$ _____	$ _____
Supplies	$ _____	$ _____
Stationery and Business Cards	$ _____	$ _____
Insurance	$ _____	$ _____
Networking Club and Professional Society Dues	$ _____	$ _____
Education (e.g., seminars, books, professional journals)	$ _____	$ _____
Business Car (e.g., payments, gas, repairs, insurance)	$ _____	$ _____
Marketing	$ _____	$ _____
Postage	$ _____	$ _____
Entertainment	$ _____	$ _____
Repair, Cleaning, Maintenance and Laundry	$ _____	$ _____
Travel	$ _____	$ _____
Business Loan Payments	$ _____	$ _____
Licenses and Permits	$ _____	$ _____
Salary/Draw*	$ _____	$ _____
Staff Salaries/Payroll Expenses	$ _____	$ _____
Taxes	$ _____	$ _____
Professional Fees	$ _____	$ _____
Decorations	$ _____	$ _____
Furniture and Fixtures	$ _____	$ _____
Equipment	$ _____	$ _____
Inventory	$ _____	$ _____
Other	$ _____	$ _____
TOTAL MONTHLY	$ _____	
TOTAL YEARLY		$ _____

In most instances it's not wise or appropriate to take draw for the first 6-12 months.

Marketing Forms

Target Market Analysis

Target market group title:

• Applicable Demographics

  Age

  Income level

  Occupation

  Gender

  Geographic location

  Educational level

  Other

• Target's physical, emotional and personal needs and goals

• Features your practice offers*

• Benefits your services provide*

- Places to find members of this market

  Stores where they shop

  Places where they socialize

  Online newsgroups

  Other

- Publications they read

  Local and national magazines

  Print newsletters

  Online newsletters

- Groups they belong to

  Support groups

  Civic organizations

  Professional associations

  Social clubs

- Special events and important dates

  Specific awareness days

  Races (for athletes)

  Seasonal stresses (e.g., January - April for accountants)

- Companies and wellness providers who service this market

- Trends that will most likely affect this market

- Where they look for help

  Online resources

  Telephone book

  Bulletin boards

  Friends

  Organizations

  Other

- Needs that aren't being met by traditional services and products

  This could range from physical relief from current condition to emotional components such as

  compassion and understanding

Client Forms

Health History

Check the following conditions that apply to you, past and present. Please add your comments to clarify the condition.

Musculo-Skeletal
- ❏ Headaches
- ❏ Joint stiffness/swelling
- ❏ Spasms/cramps
- ❏ Broken/fractured bones
- ❏ Strains/sprains
- ❏ Back, hip pain
- ❏ Shoulder, neck, arm, hand pain
- ❏ Leg, foot pain
- ❏ Chest, ribs, abdominal pain
- ❏ Problems walking
- ❏ Jaw pain/TMJ
- ❏ Tendinitis
- ❏ Bursitis
- ❏ Arthritis
- ❏ Osteoporosis
- ❏ Scoliosis
- ❏ Bone or joint disease
- ❏ Other: _____

Circulatory and Respiratory
- ❏ Dizziness
- ❏ Shortness of breath
- ❏ Fainting
- ❏ Cold feet or hands
- ❏ Cold sweats
- ❏ Swollen ankles
- ❏ Pressure sores
- ❏ Varicose veins
- ❏ Blood clots
- ❏ Stroke
- ❏ Heart condition
- ❏ Allergies
- ❏ Sinus problems
- ❏ Asthma
- ❏ High blood pressure
- ❏ Low blood pressure
- ❏ Lymphedema
- ❏ Other: _____

Skin
- ❏ Rashes
- ❏ Allergies
- ❏ Athlete's Foot
- ❏ Warts
- ❏ Moles
- ❏ Acne
- ❏ Cosmetic surgery
- ❏ Other: _____

Digestive
- ❏ Nervous stomach
- ❏ Indigestion
- ❏ Constipation
- ❏ Intestinal gas/bloating
- ❏ Diarrhea
- ❏ Diverticulitis
- ❏ Irritable bowel syndrome
- ❏ Crohn's Disease
- ❏ Colitis
- ❏ Adaptive aids
- ❏ Other: _____

Nervous System
- ❏ Numbness/tingling
- ❏ Twitching of face
- ❏ Fatigue
- ❏ Chronic pain
- ❏ Sleep disorders
- ❏ Ulcers
- ❏ Paralysis
- ❏ Herpes/shingles
- ❏ Cerebral Palsy
- ❏ Epilepsy
- ❏ Chronic Fatigue Syndrome
- ❏ Multiple Sclerosis
- ❏ Muscular Dystrophy
- ❏ Parkinson's disease
- ❏ Spinal cord injury
- ❏ Other: _____

Reproductive System
- ❏ Pregnancy:
  - ❏ Current ❏ Previous
- ❏ PMS
- ❏ Menopause
- ❏ Pelvic Inflammatory Disease
- ❏ Endometriosis
- ❏ Hysterectomy
- ❏ Fertility concerns
- ❏ Prostate problems

Other
- ❏ Loss of appetite
- ❏ Forgetfulness
- ❏ Confusion
- ❏ Depression
- ❏ Difficulty concentrating
- ❏ Drug use _____
- ❏ Alcohol use _____
- ❏ Nicotine use _____
- ❏ Caffeine use _____
- ❏ Hearing impaired
- ❏ Visually impaired
- ❏ Burning upon urination
- ❏ Bladder infection
- ❏ Eating disorder
- ❏ Diabetes
- ❏ Fibromyalgia
- ❏ Post/Polio Syndrome
- ❏ Cancer
- ❏ Infectious disease (please list)

- ❏ Other congenital or acquired disabilities (please list)_____

- ❏ Surgeries _____
- ❏ Other: _____

For clients who need mobility assistance, please give your
height: _____ weight: _____

Please list any additional comments regarding your health and well-being: _____

_____

I have stated all conditions that I am aware of and this information is true and accurate. I will inform the health care provider of any changes in my status.

Client's Signature: _____ Date: _____

PHYSICAL ACTIVITY READINESS QUESTIONNAIRE (PAR-Q)

Name: _____ Signature: _____ Date: _____

PAR-Q is designed to help you help yourself. Many health benefits are associated with regular exercise, and the completion of the PAR-Q is a sensible first step to take if you are planning to increase the amount of physical activity in your life.

For most people activity should not pose any problem or hazard. PAR-Q has been designed to identify the small number of adults for whom physical activity might be inappropriate or for those who should have medical advice concerning the type of activity most suitable for them.

Common sense is your best guide in answering these few questions. Please read them carefully and check the correct answer opposite the question if it applies to you.

YES   NO

___ ___ 1. Had your doctor ever said you have heart trouble?

___ ___ 2. Do you frequently have pains in your heart and chest?

___ ___ 3. Has a doctor ever told you that you have a bone or joint problem, such as arthritis, that might be made worse by exercise?

___ ___ 4. Has your doctor ever said your blood pressure was too high or low?

___ ___ 5. Is there a good physical reason not mentioned here why you should not follow an activity program even if you wanted to follow one?

___ ___ 6. Do you even feel faint or have spells of severe dizziness?

___ ___ 7. Are you over age 65 and not accustomed to vigorous exercise?

YES to one or more questions

If you have not recently done so, consult with your personal physician by telephone or in person before increasing your physical activity and/or taking a fitness evaluation. Tell your physical what questions you answered "YES" to on this PAR-Q or present your PAR-Q copy.

PROGRAMS
After medical evaluation, seek advice from your physician as to your suitability for
-Unrestricted physical activity starting off easily and progressing gradually, and
-Restricted or supervised activity to meet your specific goals

---

NO to all questions
If you answer the PAR-Q accurately, you have reasonable assurance of your present suitability for
-A graduated exercise program – a gradual increase in proper exercise to promote good fitness & development
-A final evaluation

POSTPONE – Always postpone when you have a minor illness such as a cold

HIPAA Forms

CONSENT FOR THE USE AND DISCLOSURE OF HEALTH INFORMATION (HIPAA) FORM

I understand that, by signing this Consent form:

- I am giving my consent for the use and disclosure of my health and session information to carry out _____ sessions at

_____

- I am giving my consent for this information to be shared amongst the following parties, for the purpose above:

List of who sees information

_____

_____

Client Name:_____

Signature:_____ Date: _____

If this Consent is signed by a personal representative on behalf of the client, complete the following:

Personal Representative's Name: _____

Signature: _____ Date: _____

Relationship to Client: _____

Disclaimer: We make every effort to enforce professional ethics and boundaries in all matters relating to clients, their health and their information.